Succulents

A Wisley handbook

Clive Innes

Cassell

The Royal Horticultural Society

Cassell Educational Limited
Artillery House, Artillery Row
London SW1P 1RT
for the Royal Horticultural Society

First published 1989

British Library Cataloguing in Publication Data

Innes, Clive
  1. Succulents.
  Succulents.
  I. Title II. Series
  582.1′4

  ISBN 0-304-32196-6

Photographs by Clive Innes and Michael Warren
Line drawings by Maureen Holt
Design by Lesley Stewart

Phototypesetting by Chapterhouse,
The Cloisters, Formby
Printed in Hong Kong by Wing King Tong Co. Ltd

Succulents

Cover: the spectacular flowers of *Adenium obesum* have earned it the name of desert rose

Overleaf: the hybrids of *Portulaca grandiflora* make a colourful addition to any garden (both photographs by Clive Innes)

Contents

Introduction	7
What is a succulent?	9
Leaf succulents	9
Stem succulents	10
Root succulents	10
Distribution	12
Cultivation	14
Compost	14
Watering	14
Feeding	15
Containers	15
Light	15
Temperature	15
Succulents for different situations	16
In the home	16
In the greenhouse	16
Outdoors	18
Propagation	19
Seed	19
Cuttings and offsets	20
Directory of succulent plants	24
A note on classification	24
Agavaceae (including Dracaenaceae)	24
Apocynaceae	27
Asclepiadaceae	28
Commelinaceae	32
Compositae (Asteraceae)	33
Convolvulaceae	34
Crassulaceae	35
Cucurbitaceae	40
Euphorbiaceae	40
Geraniaceae	41
Liliaceae (Aloeaceae)	43
Mesembryanthemaceae	45
Moraceae	50

Agave victoriae-reginae is one of the finest species in the genus

Passifloraceae	50
Pedaliaceae	51
Portulacaceae	51
Vitaceae	52
Pests and diseases	55
Pests	55
Diseases	57
Further information	59
Suppliers	59
Recommended reading	59
Societies	60
Index of genera	62

Introduction

The plants commonly termed "succulents" are so numerous that it would prove a mammoth task even to consider an introduction to them all. Over 50 different plant families include genera in which succulents are represented, with about 12 families containing the more familiar and easily available species. This book, therefore, concentrates on those succulents most likely to be encountered, with the major exception of cacti (to which a separate Wisley handbook is devoted). The omission may be justified because the Cactaceae, although it is one of the four main families of succulents, is distinguished from all the others by having a peculiar growing point called an areole, a small cushion-like growth from which develop spines, flowers and branches.

Many succulents have an unusual appearance and are often confused with cacti – an understandable mistake when one considers the resemblance of several euphorbias to cacti. It is hoped that this book will be useful in explaining any particular characteristics which help to identify succulents and that in general it will provide enough basic information to enable the beginner to grow these very attractive plants successfully.

Succulents are decorative, adaptable, not difficult culturally and can be a pleasant addition to the home. Equally, in a greenhouse they can ensure a colourful and intriguing display throughout the year. They have a place in the garden too. Many species are relatively hardy in Britain and some, notably sedums and sempervivums, are commonly grown as alpines in gardens. Other well-known succulents are the annual *Portulaca grandiflora* in its many coloured forms and the Livingstone daisy, *Dorotheanthus bellidiformis*, whose decorative flowers adorn gardens during the summer months. We have become accustomed to seeing the yucca as a garden plant and the agave also, particularly in southern Britain.

Conservation and the need to ensure the survival of plants in their habitat have at least gained well-deserved prominence. It is worthy of note that many succulents which find their way into cultivation, for instance, *Euphorbia obesa*, *Luckhoffia* and *Aloe variegata*, are almost extinct in the wild. It is the duty of those who possess such plants to treasure them and propagate them, so that they are not lost to posterity. Fortunately, numerous societies exist worldwide to encourage interest in succulents and promote their conservation, including the British Cactus and Succulent

7

Luckhoffia beukmanii, from Cape Province, South Africa, has become very rare in its native habitat

Society, which is open to all enthusiasts. Nature reserves and national and regional parks have also become a necessary and welcome feature in countries where succulent plant populations were being decimated.

The growing of succulents can become an absorbing hobby, but it is necessary to take certain precautions. Never buy a plant just for the name: names change often and you could well discover that your purchase is already in your collection under another label. When buying a plant, examine it thoroughly and make sure it is in good condition – free from pests, clean-looking and not pale and straggly. There are many specialist nurseries and reputable plant centres which stock a wide range of succulents and they frequently offer a mail-order service, if you cannot visit in person. Seed of named species is also obtainable from a number of sources (see p.59).

What is a succulent?

Broadly defined, a succulent is a plant capable of withstanding long periods of drought. It is equipped to survive such adverse conditions by the ability to store moisture – in the leaves, the stem or the rootstock – and this feature is evident in all the thousands of succulent plants known to man.

LEAF SUCCULENTS

In these species, nearly the whole leaf constitutes the water storage tissue and is entirely enveloped in a thin layer of assimilating tissue, for absorbing water and carbon dioxide and converting them to food. With certain of the family Mesembryanthemaceae, the leaf structure has been reduced to a small evaporative area, often with just two "leaves" almost fused together in a rounded fleshy body, as in *Lithops* and *Conophytum*. With other genera, such as *Echeveria*, *Aloe* and *Agave*, the fleshy leaves have become more or less compacted in the form of a rosette, thus affording protection from the evaporating effect of the rays of the sun. Finally, with succulents like *Crassula* and *Kalanchoe*, the leaves may be set at intervals along the stems and are noticeably fleshy, with a coating of tough wax-like skin to discourage evaporation. (See figure 1.)

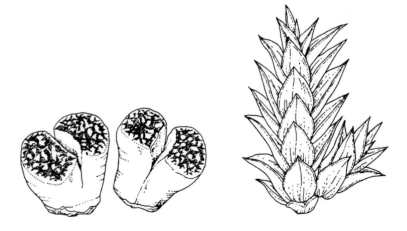

Figure 1: examples of leaf succulents – *Lithops* (left) and *Haworthia viscosa* (right)

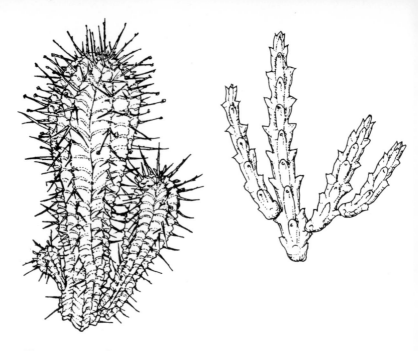

Figure 2: examples of stem succulents – *Euphorbia horrida* (left) and *Orbea* (Stapelia) *variegata* (right)

STEM SUCCULENTS

These plants are generally almost or totally leafless and what leaves they have tend to fall quickly. The absence of leaves actually provides against transpiration or loss of moisture through evaporation. Leafless succulents are invariably of very fleshy texture and the water storage tissue is concentrated in the fresh green stems and shoots (and also in the small leaves which may develop temporarily in some species). Hence, the functions of transpiration and assimilation, which are normally undertaken by the leaves, are the prime responsibility of the shoots and stems, so guaranteeing the survival of the plant. Many stem succulents have angled shoots, for instance, *Euphorbia*, *Stapelia* and *Caralluma*, as an additional precaution against excessive evaporation; the shoots not only have the protective skin, but with some species there is also a fine wax-like covering or a coating of minute hairs. (See figure 2.)

ROOT SUCCULENTS

These succulents have a thick, fleshy, mostly tuberous rootstock, which provides a reservoir of nourishment for the plant. (See figure 3.) The tuberous roots may be large, small round or elongated, the latter often in the form of a lengthy taproot, although a few plants, for example, *Boweia*, possess more of a bulbous base. With all these succulents, the water storage tissue is mainly confined to the rootstock. In certain cases, such as *Pachypodium*, the stems arise directly from the tuberous rootstock. This often develops into a thick, fleshy, rounded, swollen base at, or slightly below, ground level, which is termed a caudex. The caudex may be coated with a thick tough skin, or frequently has a corky or woody surface, protecting the water storage tissue and

Figure 3: example of root succulents – *Ceropegia woodii*

11

The stems of *Pachypodium rosulatum* var. *gracilis* (left) emerge directly from the caudex; the crown of thorns, *Euphorbia milii* (right), is one of the best known representatives of the genus

enabling the plant to withstand long periods of drought. Many of the Cucurbitaceae family have distinctive caudices and there is something of a "caudiciform cult" among enthusiasts for these unusual plants.

DISTRIBUTION

Succulents have a worldwide distribution. Some – *Sedum*, *Sempervivum*, *Chiastophyllum* and the like – are to be found in northern Europe. More are encountered in temperate zones of southern Europe, parts of China and Japan, notably *Orostachys*, a few *Caralluma*, many *Sedum* and other low-growing plants. By far the greatest number, however, inhabit the tropical and sub-tropical regions of the world and species of the same genus are often widely dispersed across them. Thus *Kalanchoe* is native to Africa, including Madagascar, as well as the West Indies and other areas of the New World, while *Euphorbia* is represented on every continent, the obvious characteristics of shape, size and general structure varying according to habitat. Members of the family Asclepiadaceae abound from the Himalayan regions to parts of Australia, with *Hoya* species at the two extremes, and

12

there are untold species of *Stapelia, Caralluma, Huernia, Hoodia, Ceropegia* and other genera in the vast African complex between.

The Americas are basically the home of *Agave, Yucca, Echeveria, Dudleya* and several other popular genera and even a number of *Sedum* species occur in the USA and Mexico. *Jatropha* are virtually confined to America and the West Indies. Africa in its entirety houses the majority of succulent plants and many of them, such as *Aloe, Haworthia* and *Gasteria*, are found only there. The numerous species within the family Mesembryanthemaceae are almost exclusive to Africa, with a very few exceptions in Australia and elsewhere. The genus *Pelargonium* too is largely African, most of the species being from the south of the country.

A knowledge of the habitats of succulent plants – the rainy and dry seasons that they experience, the altitudes at which they grow, their flowering periods and whether they have to accept long periods of drought or enjoy more kindly conditions during the year – is helpful in understanding how to care for them in cultivation. The most important factor in successful growing is to really know your plants.

Xanthorrhoea semiplana grows very large in its natural habitat

Cultivation

There are certain guidelines to follow when growing succulent plants, whether in the home or greenhouse, or even outdoors (see p.18).

COMPOST

With very few exceptions, a mixture composed of these ingredients (by volume) will achieve good results:

1 part good sterilized loam
2 parts finely shredded sphagnum peat
1 part sharp, gritty, washed sand
plus a sprinkling of slow-release fertilizer or, even better, a little thoroughly decomposed cow manure

Unfortunately, good uncontaminated loam is now scarce and expensive. The alternative to the home-made mixture is to buy a specially prepared cactus compost or a commercially produced soilless compost. The cactus compost is equally suitable for most other succulents and should already contain sufficient gritty sand, but if it seems too retentive of moisture, add a little more. With soilless compost it is necessary to incorporate small, washed, gritty sand, to make up a third or slightly more of the total bulk. It is also possible to use John Innes potting compost No. 2, again providing additional washed, gritty sand.

It is essential to include gritty sand in the compost in order to obtain a very porous mixture, for succulents cannot tolerate wet feet and will quickly rot.

WATERING

Succulents should be watered only during the period of active growth, which varies according to the plant concerned. Water the compost thoroughly when it is dry, then wait until it has almost dried out again before giving more water. Little doses whether the plants needs it or not can be harmful. Remember that no water is required during the dormant season. Generally speaking, this coincides with the winter months in Britain, from early November to March, although there are exceptions, as noted in the directory (pp.24–51).

FEEDING

The supply of nutrients in a prepared compost lasts for a limited time and succulents should therefore be fed at roughly monthly intervals during the growing and flowering seasons. General-purpose fertilizers, containing nitrogen and potash, as well as the essential trace elements like iron, magnesium, manganese, boron, copper and molybdenum, are suitable. They are available in liquid form or as a soluble powder to be added to the water.

CONTAINERS

Clay or plastic containers may be used, although plastic has the advantage of being easier to keep clean and tends to dry out less rapidly than clay. The size of pot is important and should be selected to allow room for the roots of the plant to spread without being cramped or, in the case of a plant with a taproot, to provide sufficient depth for root growth. If a plant is under-potted, it will soon begin struggling. At the other extreme, if it is over-potted, the plant may look ridiculous and can have too much damp soil around the rootstock during the growing season, which inhibits the drying-out process. Always crock the container well, placing a layer of broken pot, gravel or similar material at the bottom to assist drainage.

Repotting is required only when the roots start to protrude through the base of the pot or become very obvious on the surface of the compost. It is usually best carried out in early spring.

LIGHT

Most succulents will take full sun or, at least, bright light, although there are exceptions (see the directory, pp.24–51). As before, it helps to know something about their origin – whether from open arid country, like most of the Mesembryanthemaceae family, or protected from the blistering effect of the sun's rays by other plant life, as with members of the Commelinaceae – so that you can place them in the best position.

TEMPERATURE

It is wise to maintain a minimum temperature of 55°F (13°C) for the majority of succulents and with many of them a slightly higher temperature will prove beneficial.

Succulents for different situations

IN THE HOME

A number of succulents have had a place of honour as house-plants for very many years, often without the owner even being aware they were succulents. *Hoya* and *Sansevieria* are two which come to mind; there are also the partridge-breasted aloe, *Aloe variegata*, and the numerous hybrids of *Kalanchoe blossfeldiana*, with their long-lasting flowers in many beautiful shades, which have become popular more recently. However, the majority of succulent plants, not just a chosen few, can be grown very successfully indoors, so long as they are given a bright position, away from draughts, and normal procedures for watering and feeding are followed.

One other point may be mentioned: it is often assumed that plants should be watered from below, standing the pot in water until it has taken its fill. This can be done, always remembering to tip away any surplus water afterwards, but it is not really necess-ary. Plants can just as easily be watered from above, which also helps to keep them free from dust. Do not water in the heat of the day, when there is a danger of burns from the combination of sun-shine and drops of water on the plants.

IN THE GREENHOUSE

Those who have the benefit of a greenhouse can provide ideal conditions for growing succulents, especially some of the larger ones which may be difficult to accommodate in the home. First and foremost, the greenhouse must be sound and weatherproof and free from draughts. Good ventilation is essential to prevent stagnation and can be achieved with roof and side vents. Fans can be introduced if necessary to improve the air circulation.

Succulents must have good light throughout the year and therefore the greenhouse should be in an open sunny location and the glass must be kept really clean. However, certain species need protection from full sun, otherwise they might be scorched, and should have some sort of shading, for instance, green netting,

Opposite, above: *Kalanchoe blossfeldiana* is familiar as a houseplant

Below: the beauty of the Mesembryanthemaceae, one of the largest succulent families

slats or white shading painted on the outside of the glass. Heating will be required to maintain the correct temperature. The safest and most efficient system for a small greenhouse is an electrically controlled convector, which distributes warm air to every corner of the structure and does not emit harmful fumes. (See also the Wisley handbook, *The small greenhouse*.)

OUTDOORS

A number of succulents can be successfully grown outdoors, particularly sedums and sempervivums, most of which are completely hardy. They are popular alpine plants and do well in a rock garden, raised bed or trough. The well-known century plant, *Agave americana*, also thrives in gardens in the mild south and west of Britain; in colder districts it may be grown in a large container and placed outside in the summer. Yuccas can be treated in the same way. As bedding plants raised from seed, *Dorotheanthus bellidiformis* and *Portulaca grandiflora* provide carpets of colour in a sunny flower bed.

Succulents grown outdoors are best planted on a slope, to maximize drainage, in a sunny open position. They appreciate some protection from wind and rain and can be placed against a south-facing wall or, better still, in the shelter of a roof overhang. Garden soil usually meets their requirements, especially if it is reasonably light and porous.

Most pot-grown succulents will benefit from a period in the open air. Choose a time in late spring or summer when the weather is congenial and place them, still in their pots, in a light draught-free position outside, though not necessarily in full sun. Remember that they will need regular watering.

The recently discovered *Graptopetalum bellum*

Propagation

There are several ways to increase a collection of succulents, all of which present very few obstacles.

SEED

Seed is the obvious first choice and is a particularly useful method with some of the less common species, which are not so readily available as plants from commercial sources. It has the further merit of being economical and of producing plants which, from the moment of germination, become adjusted to the conditions in which they will be grown. With due care, seed-grown plants can make excellent mature specimens, so long as their essential requirements are met.

To prepare for sowing, select a suitable seed tray or pot, completely cover the base with a shallow layer of small gravel to prevent waterlogging and fill with a gritty seed compost to within $\frac{1}{2}$ in. (1 cm) of the top. Firm well to make a level surface. For very fine, almost dust-like seeds, spread a thin layer of sharp small grit over the compost surface and carefully sprinkle the seeds on top, but do not cover the compost. Larger seeds should be set on top of the prepared compost and covered with a layer of gritty sand the same depth as the size of the seeds. Then lightly spray the compost, using tepid water if possible, until it is evenly moist; alternatively, stand the seed tray in a bowl of tepid water until the surface of the compost is visibly moist and allow it to drain. Cover with a sheet of glass, paper or both and keep in a semi-shady but warm place, in a heated propagator if available. Generally speaking, a temperature of 70°F (21°C) is sufficient throughout the germination period. Germination may take only a few days, or sometimes weeks, even months, so don't despair if seeds fail to produce results as quickly as you hoped!

Once the seeds have germinated, remove the glass, but leave the paper on for a little longer, and place the container in a slightly brighter position. Gradually acclimatize the seedlings as they develop, giving more light and always ensuring plenty of air, but without draughts. Keep the compost just moist, not wet, and maintain at the same temperature as for germination. Feeding every two weeks or so is advisable to strengthen the seedlings.

Seeds are best sown early in the year, allowing them several months to progress before it becomes necessary to provide a

period of dormancy. The seedlings benefit from being left un-
disturbed for at least six months, or even longer, and should only
be pricked out after dormancy, at the start of the growing season.
Plants will usually flower after the second year, although this
depends on the species concerned.

CUTTINGS AND OFFSETS

Many succulents can be multiplied by leaf cuttings, particularly
members of the family Crassulaceae. Carefully remove a leaf from
the stem and allow the cut area to dry off. This drying process,
which allows a callus or seal to form, is important with all
cuttings and may take two or three days. Then insert the base of
the leaf into a fine gritty compost so that it is just supported, using
a small thin stick if necessary to hold it. Keep the cutting barely
moist, well shaded and in a temperature of 70°F (21°C). Rooting
may occur in a couple of weeks, but often takes longer. Do not
disturb the cutting until it is well established and actively
growing. (See figure 4.)

Stem cuttings can be treated in much the same way. Make the
cutting just below a node or leaf axil of the stem, allow the cut
section to dry, then insert it in a sandy compost and firm the
compost around the node, supporting if necessary. With most
succulents, for example, the Euphorbiaceae, Asclepiadaceae and
certain other families, a cutting can be taken off a branch where it
joins the stem. Give time for the cutting to dry before proceeding
as for a stem cutting. (See figures 5 and 6.)

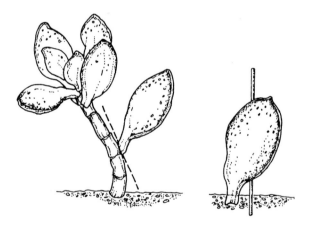

Figure 4: leaf cutting of *Crassula* – taking the cutting (left) and
inserting it (right)

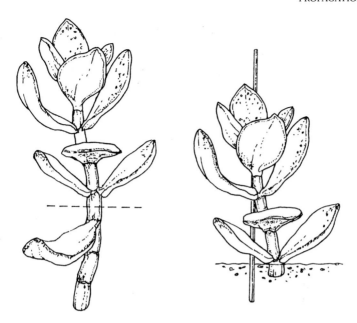

Figure 5: stem cutting of *Crassula* – taking the cutting (left) and inserting it (right)

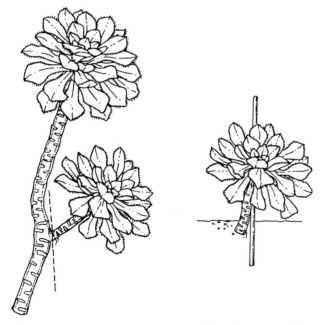

Figure 6: side stem cutting of *Aeonium* – taking the cutting (left) and inserting it (right)

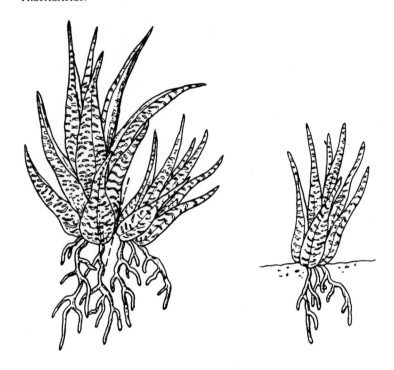

Figure 7: root cutting of *Haworthia* – detaching the rooted offset (left) and inserting it (right)

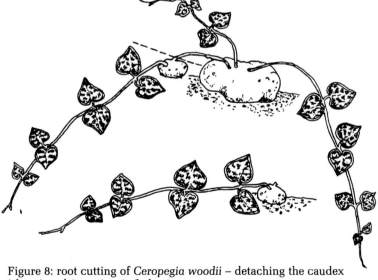

Figure 8: root cutting of *Ceropegia woodii* – detaching the caudex (above) and inserting it (below)

Ceropegia woodii can be propagated from the rounded tuberous rootstock

Offsets are common in a great number of species. In many instances, they have roots already attached and can be removed from the parent, potted separately and grown on as mature plants. Those without apparent roots should be dealt with in the same way as stem cuttings. (See figure 7.)

Succulents with a tuberous or stoloniferous rootstock, such as *Ceropegia*, *Aloe* and *Sansevieria*, provide another method of propagation. Sever a tuber or a section of the stolon, first ensuring that it possesses a growing point. Always allow the cut piece to dry, otherwise it might rot when planted. Plant in extra gritty compost, keep at a temperature of 70°F (21°C) and, once new growth becomes evident, grow on in the normal conditions for an established plant. (See figure 8.)

Cuttings should only be taken during the growing period, using healthy parts of the plant. Make sure that the knife is really sharp and clean. It is a wise precaution against disease to dust the cut with a fungicidal powder.

Directory of succulent plants

It would be impossible to encompass all succulents within the scope of this book and it is therefore confined to the better-known families and the genera and species contained therein, all of which are fairly freely available. Most will undoubtedly be familiar to succulent plant enthusiasts, although a few less common species have been included, in the hope of encouraging collectors to seek out the unusual. None of the plants described can be considered difficult to grow, especially if the general guidelines on cultivation are followed (see pp.14–18). Many are excellent plants for beginners, being both easily cultivated and readily obtainable, and these are indicated in the directory with an asterisk (*). Any particular demands of a genus or species will, of course, be explained where appropriate.

A NOTE ON CLASSIFICATION

In this directory the plants are grouped in families, which are given in alphabetical order, starting with Agavaceae and ending with Vitaceae. (An index of genera appears on pp. 60–61)

For those unfamiliar with the terminology, a plant family is an assembly of genera sharing certain botanical characteristics; the cactus family, for instance, consists of over 100 genera, all distinguished by the possession of an areole or special growing point. Family names (with only three exceptions) end in "-aceae", as in Crassulaceae, Liliaceae and so on. Each genus (plural – genera) within a family groups together species that have a peculiar affinity with each other, even though they may differ greatly in appearance; thus the spurges, members of the genus *Euphorbia*, all contain a milky sap. Finally, each species within a genus takes the generic name, rather like a surname, followed by its own specific name, like a "'given" name or Christian name, which often conveys its characteristics or origin; *Euphorbia canariensis*, for example, is native to the Canary Islands.

AGAVACEAE

This is an important family of rosette-forming plants of relatively easy culture. Some become very large and can quickly outgrow their allotted space in the greenhouse or home, so careful selection is necessary. Several are hardy and these will be noted.

Agave americana var. *marginata* has become naturalized along the Mediterranean coast

A really open, porous compost is important. Water moderately throughout the growing season. A temperature of 50°F (10°C) is sufficient for all those described below. They are summer-flowering. Propagation is from offsets or seed. (A reclassification has placed *Dracaena* and *Sanseveria* in the new family Dracaenaceae.)

Agave americana, the century plant, is probably native to Mexico, which is the centre of population for this American genus, and has become naturalized in many parts of the world. It has thick, outspreading, glaucous green, spiny edged leaves, which can attain 6½ ft (2 m) in length, each with a prominent spine at the end. The spikes of yellowish green flowers appear only when the plant is large and mature, reaching 20 ft (6 m) or more in sub-tropical regions, after which the main rosette dies (a feature of all agaves). It should be noted that this species becomes very big with age and could be an embarrassment in the average greenhouse. However, it can be planted outdoors in a protected spot, especially in southern Britain. Popular varieties include *mediopicta*, with a wide yellow stripe down the centre of the greyish green leaves; *mediopicta* forma *alba*, which has a white band in the middle and is generally a more compact, smaller plant; and the well-known *marginata*,* with yellow margins to the greenish leaves.

A. filifera is a large widespreading rosette up to about 20 in. (50 cm) high. The dark green leaves have white markings and numerous curved, whitish threads at the edges. The flowers are greenish purple or yellowish green with long stamens.

A. stricta has many slender, stiff, tapering leaves some 1 ft (30 cm) long, which form a neat, dense, erect rosette. The flowers are borne on a 6½ ft (2 m) stem.

Calibanus hookeri, a curious plant with a distinctive caudex, which is its main attraction

A. utahensis, a native of mountainous areas of the USA, has several varieties. They are low plants rarely exceeding 1 ft (30 cm) across, with greyish green, spiny edged leaves. Particularly attractive is the variety *eborispina*, which has more greyish leaves, each with a long greyish white terminal spine.

A. victoriae-reginae is one of the finest agaves. The dense rosette is made up of incurved, dark green, white-patterned leaves, distinctly ridged on the under-surface and up to 6 in (15 cm) long. There are a number of varieties (see p. 6).

Calibanus hookeri comes from Mexico, where it is scarcely distinguishable from the surrounding grassland. It is an interesting caudiciform plant, with a large caudex reaching 1 ft (30 cm) or more in diameter and covered in a corky bark. In cultivation the caudex is visible above the compost and from it sprout long, coarse, tough, grass-like leaves. The inconspicuous flowers are pinkish purple.

Dracaena draco is native to the Canary Islands and representative of a few members of this genus which are truly succulent. The sword-shaped leaves are glaucous green and reddish at the base, forming loose rosettes at the tips of the branches. The dragon tree, as it is called, is said to live to a great age and can be easily grown from seed, flowering after only a few years. It is an excellent houseplant.

Sansevieria cylindrica originates from west Africa and has completely cylindrical, deep green leaves tapering to a hard tip. The white flowers are produced on a tall spike 3 ft (90 cm) high.

An example of *Dracaena draco* growing in Tenerife; it is reputed to be 1,000 years old

S. trifasciata, also from west Africa, has a rhizomatous rootstock and each shoot carries about six stiff, flat, green leaves banded with pale greenish lines. The variety *laurentii,** which is a popular houseplant, has leaves with white or yellow stripes along the edges (see p. 54).

Yucca baccata from Arizona and California has a stiff erect rosette of leaves about 3 ft (90 cm) long, edged with whitish fibres and a terminal spine. The flowers are white. Like many yuccas, it is almost hardy and flourishes outside in the mild southwest of Britain.

Y. brevifolia, the Joshua tree, is widely distributed in the southern USA and northern Mexico. It develops a long trunk with a number of branches, each ending in a smallish rosette of narrow leaves.

Y. texanum from Texas has very slender, greyish green leaves with long thread-like hairs along their length. The flower spike, over $3\frac{1}{4}$ ft (1 m) high, bears large lily-like flowers and the rootstock is slightly tuberous and stoloniferous. It is a most attractive plant, but somewhat uncommon.

APOCYNACEAE

This family includes many succulent species from both the Old and New World. They have considerable appeal for enthusiasts,

27

especially those plants with a caudex. The majority are tropical and consequently require greater care in cultivation, although several make good houseplants. A rich porous compost is essential, together with regular feeding and careful watering during the growing season. A minimum temperature of 61°F (16°C) is advisable, even during the dormant period. They flower in summer. Propagation is usually by seed.

Adenium obesum is found in many parts of Africa and in Saudi Arabia, with several localized varieties. It has a thick fleshy caudex, often like a stout bottle-shaped trunk, which in maturity can reach 3¼ ft (1 m) or more tall. It is sometimes branching, with glossy green, oval leaves spirally arranged at the tips. The flowers give ample justification for the common name of desert rose: they are large pink to carmine-rose and more or less funnel-shaped with wide-spreading petals. It is easily raised from seed, flowering when quite young (see cover).

Pachypodium geayi reaches about 25 ft (7.5 m) high in its native Madagascar and has slender palm-like leaves about 16 in. (40 cm) long, the undersurfaces covered in minute grey hairs. Quite small plants are sometimes offered, which are ideal for indoors, but the cream-coloured flowers appear only on very mature specimens.

P. lamerei,* known as the Madagascan palm, can grow to 20 ft (6 m) high, the base of the caudex being about 2 ft (60 cm) in diameter and tending to branch from near the top. The leaves are up to 16 in. (40 cm) long, while the white flowers are about 2 in. (5 cm) across and borne on a long slender tube. Small plants are becoming available as houseplants (see p. 60).

P. namaquanum is a South African species with a long, fleshy, thick, thorny trunk or caudex, eventually up to 6½ ft (2 m) tall. The short hairy leaves, with wavy edges, are produced in tufts from the top of the trunk and maroon-red yellow-striped flowers appear from the leaf axils.

P. rosulatum is native to Madagascar and varies according to its different environments. The variety *gracilis* is a slender plant with a rounded fleshy caudex, a few small terminal leaves and deep yellow flowers (see p. 12).

Plumiera acuminata,* the frangipani tree from Central and South America, has a succulent fleshy stem and branches which exude a type of latex if punctured. The large oblong leaves are shed during dormancy, after which the beautiful flowers are produced, highly scented and dark cream with a yellow centre. The variety *rubra* is similar to the type, but has lovely carmine-red flowers with a yellow centre.

ASCLEPIADACEAE

This family contains some of the most fascinating succulents, often with extraordinary flowers, which are produced in late spring or summer. Many are low-growing, coming from semi-arid areas, while others inhabit forests, a number even being epiphytic or tree-dwelling. Unless otherwise stated, all the plants described need a bright position, although not necessarily in full sun, an open compost, very careful watering, keeping them almost dry during the rest season, and a minimum temperature of 61°F (16°C). Propagation is normally easy from seed.

Caralluma europaea is from southern Spain and North Africa. The branching,

The frangipani tree, *Plumiera acuminata* (left), is widely grown throughout the tropics for its fragrant flowers; unlike most other Asclepiadaceae, *Ceropegia haygarthii* (right) should have a partly shaded position

often prostrate stems are four-angled and greyish green with reddish markings. The flowers are greenish yellow with brown lines, carried in umbels of about ten. There are several varieties, the flowers sometimes more purplish or green with reddish marks in the centre or, in the case of the variety *simonis*, reddish brown with numerous white and brownish hairs.

C. joannis is a well-known species from Morocco, similar to *C. europaea*, except that the stems are wavy edged and finely toothed. The flowers, in clusters, are greenish yellow with reddish spots on the tube and velvety purple, brownish lobes.

C. plicatiloba is a free-branching species from Yemen and Saudi Arabia. The erect, bluish green stems are four-angled with rounded teeth. The flowers, borne in racemes, are yellowish with reddish brown markings, the edges whitish and densely covered in purple-tipped hairs.

Ceropegia dichotoma from the Canary Islands is upright, up to 2 ft (60 cm) or more tall. The stems are greyish green and the flowers yellow with a curved tube.

C. haygarthii (*C. distincta* subsp. *haygarthii*) is a native of South Africa, in particular Natal. It is a twining plant with succulent stems and small oval leaves. The slender funnel-shaped flowers have a slightly curved tube and are creamy coloured with maroon flecks and dots and a maroon interior, from the centre of which arises a thin maroon "stalk" topped with a reddish purple knob with a few whitish hairs. A semi-shaded position is necessary.

C. woodii* is sometimes called the string of hearts on account of the small heart-shaped leaves set in pairs along the wiry trailing branches. The leaves are bluish green marbled with silver and purplish on the undersides, while the tiny flowers are purplish brown with a fringe of purple hairs. It comes from South Africa and has a rounded tuberous rootstock. This is a popular houseplant and looks attractive in a hanging basket. Partial shade is advisable (see p. 23).

Diplocyatha See *Orbea*.

Duvalia pillansii from the Karroo, South Africa, has numerous thick, greenish reddish stems, which are four-angled with a few teeth along the edges and about 1 in. (2.5 cm) long. The freely produced flowers have triangular lobes, purplish brown on the upper surface, greenish below, and are pale yellowish in the middle, with a fleshy central ring which is first whitish becoming purplish.

The flowers of *Duvalia sulcata* (left) have the fleshy central disk characteristic of the genus; species of *Hoodia*, such as *H. gordonii* (right), have relatively large flowers

D. sulcata is a small prostrate species from Arabia, with pale greyish green, purple-spotted stems, four-angled and prominently toothed. The flowers are brownish red and the glossy central ring is densely covered with reddish hairs.

Hoodia bainii from Cape Province, South Africa, through to Namibia is often confused with *H. gordonii*, but lacks the small nipples in the centre of the yellowish pinkish flowers. It is a bushy plant about 8 in. (20 cm) high and has cylindrical stems with many longitudinal ribs and tubercles armed with spined tips.

H. gordonii from Namibia is up to 18 in. (45 cm) tall. The stems have regular rib-like angles along their length, which carry protuberances with woody spines. The large, almost circular flowers are pale purplish with dark reddish nipples in the centre, but are not readily produced in cultivation.

Hoya australis, an Australian species, is a climber with thick fleshy leaves of dark green, sometimes speckled whitish. The flowers, in umbels, are waxy white with a reddish centre. This is an epiphyte, requiring semi-shade and reasonable humidity, and the compost should never be allowed to dry out completely.

H. bella (*H. lanceolata* subsp. *bella*)* is a native of Burma and familiar as a houseplant. The arching stems bear small fleshy leaves and umbels consisting of eight or nine sweetly scented, waxy white flowers with rose-pink centres. It is a true epiphyte which can be grown to perfection in a hanging basket.

*H. carnosa** is another well-known species, a vigorous climber originating from China and Australia. The leaves are oval, thick and fleshy and the flowers are gathered in large, often dense umbels, being pinkish white with a red centre and fragrant. Semi-shade is advisable and it is an excellent plant for the home (see p. 61).

H. linearis is a sub-tropical epiphyte from the Himalayas. The stems and branches are very soft, slender, greyish green and pendulous, while the narrow, almost cylindrical leaves are hairy and dark green. Small, pure white flowers are borne in drooping clusters. Shade and a minimum temperature of 61°F (16°C) are essential for this species and it should be sprayed regularly in warm weather, never allowing the compost to dry out completely. It is ideal for a hanging basket.

H. purpurea-fusca from the forests of Java is a clambering or trailing plant to 13 ft (4 m) in length. The dark green leaves are often flecked with silver and the flowers, in large umbels, are reddish purple or purplish brown. A shaded position is imperative and the compost should always be slightly moist (see p. 61).

The flowers of *Hoya australis* (left) are scented of honeysuckle; the ten-pointed flower of *Huernia striata* (right), with shorter points between the main lobes, is typical of the genus

Huernia oculata from Namibia produces many reddish green stems about 4 in. (10 cm) long, five-angled and with fleshy teeth. Flowers appear from the base of the new growth and have five large and five very small lobes of dark, almost blackish red and a pure white centre.

H. schneiderana from Malawi and Mozambique has stems up to 8 in. (20 cm) long, with toothed angles. The bell-shaped flower is brownish on the outer surface and velvety, deep purple inside, the margins pinkish and edged with maroon.

H. striata has bluntly angled stems up to 3 in. (8 cm) high. The flowers are about 1 in. (2.5 cm) across, the tube greenish or maroon on the outside, yellow inside, the lobes also yellow and the whole marked with irregular, brownish maroon bands.

Luckhoffia beukmanii from Cape Province, South Africa, grows about 28 in. (70 cm) tall. The slightly hairy, greyish green stems have nine angles raised in tubercles. The large flowers, two or three together, are brownish with yellow dots or maroon red with minute yellowish spots (see p. 8).

Orbea ciliata (*Diplocyatha ciliata*) from the Karroo, South Africa, has four-angled, prominently toothed stems about 2 in. (5 cm) long. The whitish flowers, borne singly, are about 3 in. (8 cm) across; the edges of the spreading lobes are hairy and the funnel-shaped central ring has a recurved rim and is dotted with purple.

O. semota (*Stapelia semota*) from Kenya and Tanzania has stems up to 3 in. (8 cm) tall, smooth and four-angled with spreading teeth. The flowers have deep brownish lobes with paler markings and a dark brown five-angled ring edged with reddish hairs.

O. variegata (*Stapelia variegata*)* is one of the commonest of this group with beautiful, but evil-smelling flowers. The stems are about 4 in. (10 cm) high, bluntly angled, greyish green and with projecting teeth. The starfish-like flowers vary according to the variety, of which there are many. In the variety *atropurpurea*, which is very much like the species, the flower is about 3 in. (8 cm) across and the lobes have a wrinkled surface, the tips being yellow with dark brownish purple marks and the centre blackish purple with a few circular markings. It is from Cape Province, South Africa (see p. 58).

Stapelia erectiflora has slender downy stems about 6 in. (15 cm) high. The flowers are a particular feature: carried on long stalks, they are greyish purple densely covered with white hairs, only about ½ in. (1 cm) across and with the lobes rolled

The striking five-lobed flower of *Tridentea longipes* (left); a member of the Commelinaceae, *Tripogandra warscewicziana* (right) needs a semi-shaded position

right back, giving a rounded effect like a Turkish fez. Southern and central Africa is the home of the genus.

S. flavopurpurea has bluish green, four-angled stems some 2 in. (5 cm) tall. The small flowers are more or less flat and have five lobes covered with minute, purplish red wrinkles and a central white disc with many pinkish red hairs.

S. schinzii is another small plant, having four-angled, dark green, purple-mottled stems. The large flower, about 5 in. (12 cm) in diameter, has five elongated, tapering lobes, blackish purple, wrinkled and edged with purple hairs. It is a variable species, depending on the habitat.

Trichocaulon pedicellatum from the Namib desert of southwest Africa is one of the smallest members of this genus. It has cylindrical ridged stems and dark reddish brown flowers with tapering lobes, borne on short stalks from the sides of the stems.

T. pillansii from Cape Province, South Africa, can attain 7 in. (18 cm) in height. The greyish green stems have warts with bristly tips, while the bright yellow flowers have pinkish nipples just discernible on the margins.

Tridentea longipes (Stapelia longipes) comes from Namibia and is a low cushion-forming plant with smooth, bluish green stems. The purplish flowers, about 2 in. (5 cm) across, have lobes widening towards the centre, then tapering to the tips, with a wrinkled surface; they are blotched and lined with white near the throat and fringed at the edges.

COMMELINACEAE

This family contains several species which are truly succulent in stem or leaf, many of them trailing or creeping, and make ideal houseplants. A semi-shady position and fairly rich, open compost are advisable and they should be watered freely during the growing season but, in the case of the deciduous species, kept reasonably dry until new growth develops. The flowers appear in summer. They are easily propagated from cuttings or seeds.

Cyanotis lanata is a densely leaved plant from tropical Africa, with stems about 1 ft (30 cm) long and a cottony hairy appearance. The flowers, mainly purple or pink, are clustered in the upper axils of the stems. It needs plenty of moisture.

C. somaliensis, a native of Somalia and neighbouring countries, is similar. The stems and leaves are white-furry and very fleshy and the flowers blue. It is deciduous.

*Tradescantia navicularis** from Peru is possibly the most succulent member of this genus, which includes the well-known trailing houseplants called wandering Jew. The short-jointed creeping stems root at the nodes and form mats. The small boat-shaped leaves are fleshy, greyish green and minutely fringed and the flowers are purplish pink.

T. sillamontana is a deciduous species from northern Mexico. The stems are white, hairy, about 2 in. (5 cm) or more long and densely clothed with thick green leaves, coated with fine white hairs. The flowers vary from pink to mauve.

Tripogandra warscewicziana is native to Guatemala. The thick succulent stems develop a rosette of dark green, slightly recurved leaves and the long-lasting flowers of deep purple are borne in clusters on a branched head. This is a splendid plant for the home or greenhouse.

COMPOSITAE (ASTERACEAE)

The daisy family is one of the largest in the plant kingdom and embraces a great number of true succulents of all kinds – stem, leaf, root, even caudiciform. Most have the typical daisy flowers, consisting of numerous disc or ray florets densely set together and surrounded by colourful or greenish bracts. These are produced in summer. The majority are of easy culture, given a sunny position, and should be watered freely in the growing season and kept fairly dry during the remainder of the year. A temperature of 50°F (10 °C) is sufficient, unless otherwise stated. Propagation is best by cuttings.

Coreopsis gigantea is a robust fleshy plant up to 6½ ft (2 m) high. It is surmounted by a thick tuft of feathery leaves and a cluster of pale yellowish flowers, each about 3 in. (8 cm) across. It should be allowed to rest in the warmest months and be kept reasonably dry, then encouraged into growth as cooler weather arrives.

Kleinia fulgens (Senecio fulgens) from Natal is a tuberous-rooted plant with prostrate stems up to 18 in. (45 cm) long. These are pale grey and powdery, as are the pale green leaves, while the small flower heads are reddish.

K. galpinii (Senecio galpinii) grows about 2 ft (60 cm) tall, with pale greyish stems and leaves and three to four flower heads bearing pale orange-red blooms. It comes from the Transvaal.

Othonna pygmaea is a dwarf South African species. It has almost a caudex base, a very short stem bearing broad fleshy leaves, which are deciduous, and yellow flowers at the top.

O. sedifolia from Namibia is a bushy plant about 2 ft (60 cm) high and across, with thick robust stems. The somewhat cylindrical leaves are spirally arranged at the tips of the shoots and have prominent tubercles on the upper surface. The flower head has bright yellow ray florets.

*Senecio articulatus** is almost 2 ft (60 cm) high, the cylindrical stem being a series of swollen joints, greyish green with purplish markings, which are its outstanding

33

feature. The flowers are yellowish. It is found in southern Africa, like the other species described here.

S. *haworthii* grows up to 12 in. (30 cm) high. The cylindrical pointed leaves and the stems are coated with a white felt. The yellow flowers are arranged in a large head, but not always produced in cultivation.

S. *rowleyanus** has many creeping slender stems, bearing numerous, almost spherical, tiny leaves. It is known as the string of beads. The flowers are insignificant but cinnamon-scented.

S. *stapeliiformis* is an erect species, with branching angular stems. The new shoots commence underground before emerging and are purplish brown and grey with dark green markings and lines, set at intervals with small leaves, which quickly wither. The flowers, on a long stalk, are bright red.

CONVOLVULACEAE

This is a large family involving many genera and species, which are worldwide in distribution. Some are shrubs, others, like the well-known convolvulus and morning glory, are climbing or trailing and a few are even parasitic. A comparatively small number can justifiably be termed succulents and these have a thick tuberous or caudiciform rootstock. While in nature the caudex is invariably underground, in cultivation it has been found advisable to leave it exposed, with just the base anchored in the compost. Water well once new growth becomes evident and then, after the leaves and flowers have died down, withhold water until the following season. The plants flower from mid- to late summer. Temperatures may soar while they are in growth and a minimum of 50°F (10°C) is recommended when they are resting. They should be partially shaded. Propagation is by seed.

Ipomoea batatas is apparently of Indian origin, but is widely grown in tropical and sub-tropical regions for the tuberous root, which is the edible sweet potato. The prostrate, slightly fleshy stems have roughly triangular leaves up to $5\frac{1}{2}$ in. (14 cm) long, either entire or with three to five lobes. The flowers are pinkish white.

I. bolusii, a South African species, has a large rounded caudex with a greyish bark. It is a deciduous plant and the grass-like leaves rise directly from the crown of the caudex or sometimes on a short stem. The flowers are funnel-shaped, pinkish lilac and usually larger than the caudex.

I. inamoena from Namibia has a large caudex 6 in. (15 cm) or more wide, with a brownish or almost black skin. The stems are about 20 in. (50 cm) long, either prostrate or semi-erect, with thick elongated leaves, fringed on the margins. Large funnel-shaped flowers of lilac to pale pink appear from the leaf axils.

Turbina holubii from the Transvaal has a large brownish caudex, from which develops a short stem with very slender, long, deciduous leaves. The purplish pink flowers are bell-shaped, opening widely at the tips.

CRASSULACEAE

This is one of the larger families of succulent plants. In general they are of easy culture and some, such as *Sedum*, *Sempervivum*

Senecio haworthii (left) is noticeable for the pure white woolly covering on stems and leaves; the lovely flowers of *Turbina holubii* (right) have a resemblance to those of convolvulus

and certain *Echeveria* species, are even hardy if planted outdoors in very porous soil. There are very few problems with species from Europe, although those of tropical or sub-tropical origin should have a minimum temperature of 50°F (10°C) and need to be kept reasonably dry during the rest period. For most, a porous compost is advised and the containers should afford ample space for plants of trailing or spreading habit. The flowering time is spring to late summer. Propagation is by stem cuttings, offsets or seed.

Adromischus festivus (*A. cooperi*) from Cape Province, South Africa, has a very short stem carrying cylindrical or thick wedge-shaped leaves, often with wavy margins and with the lower surface much rounded, of silvery green marbled with maroon. The insignificant flowers are borne on a 10 in. (25 cm) long stem.
A. mammillaris has bluish green, waxy, spindle-shaped leaves and greenish brown flowers in summer.
Aeonium arboreum from the southern Mediterranean region grows about 3¼ ft (1 m) high, with rosettes of green leaves, 8 in. (3 cm) across, at the tips of the erect stems. The variety *atropurpurea*,* when placed in full sun, has blackish red leaves and is a splendid plant for a sunny windowsill (see p. 36).
A. nobile is found in the Canary Islands, where most other members of the genus are concentrated. It has a short-stemmed rosette about 20 in. (50 cm) across, each long, light green, sticky leaf being very succulent, with curved margins. The leafy flower head is about 20 in. (50 cm) tall, with brownish red flowers in spring, although these are not produced until the plant is some seven years old.
A. smithii has very hairy stems and branches carrying an open rosette about 4 in. (10 cm) across. The leaves are yellowish green with reddish lines along them and wavy edges and the flowers are pale yellow in early spring.
*A. tabuliforme** grows almost flattened to the rock-face in the Canary Islands. It is a completely rounded, flat rosette about 20 in. (50 cm) across, consisting of bright

Aeonium arboreum, from Morocco, is a familiar sight in Mediterranean countries, where it has become widely naturalized

green leaves, with fine hairs on the edges. Deep yellow flowers are borne on a branched head up to 2 ft (60 cm) high in spring. It offsets freely.

Cotyledon ladismithensis comes from South Africa, as do the other species mentioned here. It is a choice bushy plant up to 12 in. (30 cm) tall. The fleshy, hairy, oblong leaves are set in four opposite pairs. The flower head bears shiny yellow flowers tinged with deep orange in summer.

C. orbiculata grows over $3\frac{1}{4}$ ft (1 m) tall, with very thick, fleshy stems, freely branching. The thick oval leaves are covered entirely with a waxy white frosting and the summer flowers are yellowish red. The variety *ausana* is similar, except that the leaves have a reddish margin.

C. undulata* is a popular species, growing over 20 in. (50 cm) tall. The broad opposite leaves are coated with a silvery grey bloom and have prominently wavy margins towards the tips. A tall stem bears several nodding orange-red flowers in summer.

Crassula argentea* (*C. obliqua*) is native to southern Africa, as are the majority of the species. A tree-like plant which in the wild can attain well over $3\frac{1}{4}$ ft (1 m) in height, it has a thick fleshy stem and branches with fleshy, dark green leaves, often spotted with slightly darker green. White or pinkish white flowers are produced in profusion in late winter and early spring. It is of easy culture and excellent for the home.

C. barbata, by contrast, forms a compact, basal rosette only $1\frac{1}{2}$ in. (3–4 cm) across, of incurved, dull green leaves edged with numerous projecting hairs. The flowers are small and whitish, in late spring.

C. lactea is a low, bushy plant, with erect or semi-prostrate branches. The flattish, fleshy, long-pointed leaves are green with whitish dots, while the white scented flowers are borne in dense clusters at the ends of the stalks in early summer.

C. multicava is a freely branching species about 12 in. (30 cm) tall. The leaves may be greyish or glossy green, minutely spotted, about as long as wide. The pinkish white flowers are very small but produced in great numbers on long, curved, slender stems in summer.

C. perforata is a small shrub-like plant with woody stems and branches. The broad, greyish green leaves have many red spots, particularly near the edges, and the rather small flowers are bright yellow, appearing in early summer. The paramount feature is the chain-like effect created by the arrangement of the leaves, which seem to completely surround the slender branches.

C. rosularis has a basal rosette of many dark, glossy green leaves which taper to a point, about 3 in. (8 cm) long. The rosette produces offsets, making quite dense groups. In late spring, numerous clusters of small white flowers are carried at the ends of long stalks, which tend to branch.

C. teres is a clump-forming plant with short stems and densely compacted leaves in four rows, making short leafy columns. The leaves have transparent margins and the flowers are white, in early summer.

Dudleya farinosa, from the coast of northern California, has a short branching stem, from the tips of which develop green or white-powdered leafy rosettes up to 4 in. (10 cm) across. The branched flowers head is about 12 in. (30 cm) tall, with pale yellow flowers in summer.

Echeveria derenbergii,* a popular and well-known species, comes from Mexico, as do the other echeverias described here. It forms dense cushions of roughly cylindrical rosettes about 2½ in. (6 cm) across. The leaves are white waxy on pale green and red-tipped, the margins also being reddish. The flowers are reddish yellow, in late spring.

E. lilacina is one of the more recent introductions. Plants have short thick stems with a rosette some 6 in. (15 cm) across, consisting of brownish green leaves covered with pinkish white wax-like powder. Clusters of drooping, pinkish orange flowers are borne at the ends of long slender stems in early summer.

E. nodulosa has stems and leaves densely covered with minute nipples. It is a prostrate species with slow-growing elongated stems and branches and sometimes aerial roots. The reddish-marked leaves form a dense rosette about 5 in. (13 cm) across. The flowers are yellow with a red base, borne on a stem up to 2 ft (60 cm) long in early summer.

E. pulvinata has a lax rosette of oval leaves about 2 in. (5 cm) long, very thick and fleshy and covered with whitish hairs. The reddish flowers have prominent yellow stamens and are carried on a leafy, horizontally spreading, hairy stem in summer.

E. setosa* has a stemless rosette of closely set, dark greenish leaves covered with minute white bristles. The reddish yellow flowers are born at the top of a 12 in. (30 cm) stem and produced from midsummer to early autumn. This has played a part in some of the Echeveria hybrids which have been produced, but none can surpass the species themselves (see p. 38).

Graptopetalum bellum (Tacitus bellus)* won the admiration of plant enthusiasts when it was discovered in 1972 in the mountains of northern Mexico. It has a neat fleshy rosette about 2 in. (5 cm) in diameter and bright red star-like flowers on short stems in summer (see p. 18).

G. macdougallii, also from Mexico, is a dwarf species with a short stem and produces several offsets, each having an individual rosette of bluish leaves. The flowers are greenish white with reddish tips to the petals, appearing in late spring and early summer.

Kalanchoe beharensis is probably the tallest species in the genus, able to attain 10 ft (3 m) in height. The arrow-shaped leaves have a very fleshy blade and are up to 8 in.

Echeveria setosa (left) is easy to grow and makes offsets freely;
Kalanchoe tomentosa (right) seldom flowers in cultivation but is
attractive for its woolly covering

(20 cm) long, olive-green with greyish waxy covering and heavily toothed at the edges. The flower head is about 2 ft (60 cm) high and has small, insignificant, whitish flowers in late summer. It is native to Madagascar, along with the majority of species under consideration.

K. blossfeldiana* is a popular houseplant which has been hybridized to make many different flower colours available, from yellow to orange and pinkish to deep scarlet. Growing about 12 in. (30 cm) high, it has oblong leaves of dark glossy green, often reddish and notched at the margins. The heads of small flowers are normally reddish and produced in summer. The hybrids offered at Christmas time are mainly forced for winter flowering and are best treated as annuals. However, cuttings can be taken in early spring from those which have survived the winter (see p. 17).

K. fedtschenkoi is also popular in cultivation. The leaves are bluish green, fleshy and oblong, with the edges toothed towards the base, and the flowers are pinkish, in summer.

K. manganii,* also low-growing, has woody stems and numerous branches clad in very succulent, tiny leaves, sometimes minutely hairy. Reddish flowers hang from the spreading branches in late spring. It is an excellent houseplant.

K. marmorata from Somalia, Sudan and Kenya is usually an upright plant branching from the base. The oval leaves, about 4 in. (10 cm) long, are greyish green marbled with brownish blotches and have toothed margins. The flowers are whitish, in early summer.

K. pumila* is semi-pendent with stems and branches 8–10 in. (20–25 cm) long. The greyish green leaves are stalkless and partly notched at the edges, while the flowers are slightly drooping, urn-shaped and reddish violet, in small panicles, in late spring.

K. tomentosa* is up to 18 in. (45 cm) tall, erect, sometimes branching from the base and thickly white-felted all over. The stalkless leaves are densely set along the branches and tipped with a distinctive brown blotch. The flowers are reddish on a tall stem, in summer.

K. tubiflora* is probably the best-known member of the genus. Growing up to 3½ ft (1 m) high, it is very fleshy and produces a tall compact head of reddish purple, bell-shaped blooms in summer.

Pachyphytum oviferum* from Mexico has a short, thick, fleshy, white stem, with

38

The sugar-almond plant, *Pachyphytum oviferum* (left), has a dense white coating; the well-known ice plant, *Sedum spectabile* (right), is perfectly hardy in Britain

terminal, very succulent, oval leaves, finely powdered in white or pinkish; the leaf shape and colour have won it the common name of sugar-almond plant. The bell-shaped flowers are greenish white with a reddish centre, ten or more on a delicately curved spike, appearing in early summer.

P. viride has small, greenish purplish leaves which are semi-cylindrical, especially near the base, borne on a thick, fleshy, brownish stem about 4 in. (10 cm) high. The reddish green flowers are carried in a panicle.

Sedum adolphii originates from Mexico, as do the next two species. It is fairly bushy, with thick fleshy branches and small reddish yellow leaves. The flowers are white, in early summer.

S. frutescens is up to 32 in. (80 cm) tall and the very fleshy stem is covered with a papery bark, giving it some resemblance to a bonsai tree. The narrow leaves are edged with minute warts and the flowers are white, in early summer.

S. hintonii has a compact dense rosette of oblong, fleshy, glaucous green leaves, so densely hairy as to appear whitish. The star-like flowers are green and white with prominent reddish anthers, produced in early spring.

S. montanum is a hardy species from the European Pyrenees, which forms a thick cushion of creeping shoots and narrow, dark green or reddish leaves. It does not exceed 6 in. (15 cm), even when the golden yellow flowers are produced in summer.

*S. palmeri** from Mexico has stem and basal rosettes of broad, bluish green leaves. The star-like golden yellow flowers are borne at the end of branched heads in early spring.

S. praealtum from Mexico and Guatemala is a tall species which develops shrub-like proportions. Several stout fleshy stems over 2 ft (60 cm) high arise from the base, bearing fleshy green leaves up to 2 in. (5 cm) long and topped by panicles of bright yellow flowers in late spring and early summer. It is reasonably hardy in southern Britain.

*S. sieboldii** is the well-known hardy species from Japan. The stems are up to 9 in. (25 cm) long, reddish and prostrate, while the leaves are bluish grey, rounded and arranged in whorls of three. The flowers are pink, in late summer. The variegated form, with yellowish white blotches on the foliage, is equally popular.

*S. spectabile** from China is another familiar garden plant, often called the ice plant. It has fleshy roots, stems and leaves and is deciduous. Erect-growing up to

39

9 in. (25 cm) tall, it has oval leaves, often with toothed margins, of light waxy green. The almost flat flower head consists of many pale pink blooms in late summer. There are several interesting cultivars, such as 'Ruby Glow', with reddish leaves and red flowers, and 'Variegatum', with pale green leaves mottled yellowish white and deep pink flowers (see pp. 39 and 64).

*Sempervivum arachnoideum,** the cobweb houseleek, is a mountain plant of Europe and completely hardy in Britain. The small rosettes of green leaves are covered with densely tangled, white, cobweb-like hairs. The flowers are usually reddish, although a white form is known.

S. tectorum is a European native. The greenish leaves, sometimes tipped with reddish brown and whitish towards the base, form a rosette up to $5\frac{1}{2}$ in. (14 cm) across. In general, the flowers are pinkish or red, in summer, although there are many varieties differing in leaf and flower colour. It is hardy.

Tacitus See *Graptopetalum*.

CUCURBITACEAE

The cucumber family includes many genera from both the Old and New World. Most are annual, but it is those succulent species whose rootstock develops a caudex that capture the imagination of plant enthusiasts. Although these are perhaps more for the advanced collector, it must be stressed that they present very little difficulty in cultivation. The essential requirement is a really open compost, for in the main the caudex rests on the soil surface with the base just below, so that only the roots penetrate the compost and anchor the plant firmly. A dry resting period is imperative. They flower in summer. Propagation is from seed.

Gerrardanthus macrorhizus is a sturdy climbing species from southern and eastern Africa. It has a huge boulder-like caudex, often 2 ft (60 cm) or more across, but can be grown in a pot for several years until the size of caudex makes this impossible. The stems are semi-succulent, with roughly triangular leaves, and the brownish green flowers are followed by yellowish fruits.

Kedrostis africana from Namibia and South Africa has become fairly well known in cultivation. It is a very succulent, fleshy, white caudex which lengthens in maturity. The long stems bear rough triangular leaves about 4 in. (10 cm) long, with toothed margins, and many tendrils to support its growth. The greenish flowers are succeeded by berry-like reddish fruits.

EUPHORBIACEAE

The spurges are one of the largest families and embrace plants from weeds to exotics, including the popular poinsettia, *Euphorbia pulcherrima*. This cosmopolitan group contains many genera and in the region of 5,000 species, some of which resemble cacti. They have one thing in common – a white, often poisonous sap or latex which exudes from a cut or damaged surface. The "flower" is known as a cyathium and is a combination of often picturesque bracts and small flowers, produced from late spring to midsummer. Careful attention should be given to cultivation. A minimum temperature of 50°F (10°C) is a must, while plants from equatorial regions should be kept even warmer in winter. Water them freely in the growing season, but never allow them to have wet feet or rot can easily set in. Completely dry conditions are necessary throughout dormancy. Propagation is by seed or by cuttings of branching species.

*Euphorbia canariensis** from the Canary Islands is a variable species. The greenish stems are capable of reaching 40 ft (12 m) in the wild and branch from the base. They bear pairs of thorns at intervals along the longitudinal ribs formed by the acute angles.

*E. caput-medusae** has a short caudex bearing numerous branches, spreading almost horizontally to make a flattened rosette-like plant. The whole effect has been likened to a Medusa's head and is enhanced when the many small yellowish cyathia develop at the tips of the young branches. It and the next three species come from Cape Province, South Africa (see p. 42).

E. grandicornis is a clump-forming species with usually three-angled branches, which are irregularly constricted, wavy edged and very thorny. The small orange-yellow cyathia appear towards the ends of the branches. It is a popular and sought-after species of easy culture, but demanding of space since it can grow up to 6 ft (2 m) high in nature.

E. horrida reaches 3 ft (1 m) tall, sometimes with branches from the base. The stems are 4–5 in. (10–13 cm) thick, furrowed lengthwise to form ribs and with toothed thorny angles. The cyathia are yellow.

E. meloformis is a globular plant about 4 in. (10 cm) tall and across, greenish grey and distinctly ribbed, with the angles marked with reddish lines. The cyathium is yellowish.

*E. milii** from Madagascar is the well-known crown of thorns. It is a bushy species with thorny branches and fresh green, oblong to rounded leaves. The cyathia may be red, pink, white, yellow or variegated, depending on the variety (see p. 12).

E. obesa is a desirable species from Cape Province, South Africa, similar to *E. meloformis*, but more rounded and slightly larger. The ribs are set well apart, bearing many reddish lines and striped. It is very reminiscent of certain cacti.

*Jatropha podagrica** from Central America has a thick oblong base to the branched stem. This can reach 3¼ ft (1 m) or more high in its habitat, but is normally much shorter in cultivation – up to 16 in. (40 cm), at which stage the plant is mature and will flower. The three-lobed leaves are about 6 in. (15 cm) long, generally six to eight together at the tips of the branches. The branched flower head carries numerous bright crimson blooms (see p. 42).

Pedilanthus carinatus is a short bushy plant about 18 in. (45 cm) high. The oval leaves are set regularly along the length of the branches and bird-like pinkish and white flowers appear in clusters. It is a native of the West Indies, invariably growing close to the sea (see p. 42).

P. macrocarpus from Mexico has a thick fleshy stem over 3¼ ft (1 m) high, often branching from the base. The oval leaves are small and fleshy and deciduous. The flower head carries a few reddish cyathia, slightly resembling a small bird.

GERANIACEAE

This family contains many popular plants, in particular, the pelargoniums of the window box and the geraniums or cranesbills of

41

Above: *Euphorbia caput-medusae* (left) requires a sunny spot or the branches become elongated; *Jatropha podagrica* (right), a popular houseplant which flowers when young

Below: *Pedilanthus carinatus* (left) belongs to a genus sometimes known as slipper spurge or bird cactus; *Pelargonium barklyi* (right) is recognizable as a member of the Geraniaceae from the flowers

the garden. A large number are true succulents, mainly root or stem succulents. They require a minimum temperature of 50°F (10°C) during the winter months, when they must be kept dry. Use an open compost, with good drainage, water freely throughout the growing season and give them good light. They flower in summer. Propagation is from cuttings or seed.

Pelargonium barklyi comes from South Africa, which is the home of nearly all the species. It has a tuberous rootstock, a short stem and many small, heart-shaped leaves near ground level, which are wrinkled with deep-set veins and purplish green. The flowers are borne at the end of a stem about 12 in. (30 cm) long, five to seven in a cluster, and are creamy white veined with deep pink.

P. cotyledonis from the island of St Helena is rarely more than 12 in. (30 cm) tall. It has a thick fleshy stem and broadly oval leaves which are woolly on the under-surface when young. Pure white flowers are produced in small panicles.

P. echinatum is a tuberous species forming a caudex. The succulent stems are erect and few-branched, covered with fleshy spines, while the deciduous leaves are heart-shaped and slightly lobed, dark green above, white-hairy below. The flowers, eight to ten together, are white, pink or purplish lilac, the upper petals sometimes marked with deep carmine or purple. It grows 12–18 in. (30–45 cm) tall.

P. ensatum (*P. oblongatum*) has a small caudex set above soil level. The hairy leaves on long hairy stems appear before the umbel of flowers, which are pale yellow, striped with red. It is a choice and desirable species.

*P. tetragonum** is a popular plant with a succulent stem and branches, up to 28 in. (70 cm) tall. The stems are three to four-sided, bright green and smooth, and the leaves are broadly heart-shaped and toothed. The flower head usually carries three flowers together, rose-pink with purplish veining on long stems.

Sarcocaulon l'heritieri from Namibia is an erect branching species, with green, waxy white stems bearing small thorns and small heart-shaped leaves. The flowers are pale to bright yellow.

S. multifidum, a spreading bushy species also from Namibia, has almost horizontal branches about 4 in. (10 cm) long and no thorns. Greenish woolly leaves appear in small clusters from the tubercles on the branches. The flowers are bright pink, reddish towards the centre.

LILIACEAE (ALOEACEAE)

The lily family contains many well-known plants, such as lilies, tulips and hyacinths, as well as a large number of decidedly succulent species. With few exceptions, all the succulents are easy to grow. Many flower in late winter to early February, so it is wise to maintain a temperature of 50°F (10°C) to ensure flowering. Use an open porous compost, give good light and water moderately throughout the growing season from April to September. If suitable temperatures have been provided, an occasional watering once the flower spikes appear will not go amiss, but choose the brightest days. Propagation is by offsets or seed.

*Aloe arborescens** is from South Africa and Malawi, the African continent being the home of most aloes. This popular species has a rosette of long, fleshy, greenish leaves, 18–24 in. (45–60 cm) tall, with small teeth on the margins. It offsets freely, quickly forming large clusters. The flowers are reddish, borne on a stout stem in early spring. There is also an attractive variegated form with yellow-striped leaves.

A. aristata* is perhaps the commonest species of the genus. The small rosettes consist of many dark green leaves, which are almost totally covered with regular, minute, soft spines and have whitish edges with tiny horny teeth. Plants offset very freely, rapidly developing into large clumps. The flower spike is up to 20 in. (50 cm) long, bearing clusters of orange-red blooms in late spring and early summer.

A. distans has a creeping stem, often very extended, with a few leaves scattered along the length, but densely arranged at the tip to make an attractive firm rosette. The broadly oval leaves are fresh or bluish green, very succulent, each some 4 in. (10 cm) long and pointed at the tips; they have yellowish horny edges with teeth, which are also evident on the undersurface. The flowering stem is about 16 in. (40 cm) tall with reddish flowers, produced in early spring or sometimes before.

A. variegata,* the popular partridge-breasted aloe, is now apparently almost unknown in the wild. The erect lance-shaped leaves are deep green with white ir-regular markings and horny whitish margins. Pinkish reddish flowers are carried on a spike about 12 in. (30 cm) high from late spring to early summer.

A. zanzibarica (A. concinna) from the island of Zanzibar is a most attractive species with variegated leaves and a semi-creeping habit. It grows up to 1 ft (30 cm) tall, the leaves forming an elongated rosette. The flower stem is about 8 in. (20 cm) long and bears pale scarlet flowers with greenish edges in summer. It is a very desirable plant and easily grown but, unfortunately, like many dwarf aloes, it is uncommon.

A. zebrina has lance-shaped, fleshy, dark green leaves 6–12 in. (15–30 cm) long, covered with numerous whitish green spots which often merge into transverse bands, the margins with pale brownish teeth. The flower head may be $3\frac{1}{4}$ ft (1 m) or more tall, carrying a spike of deep red blooms in late summer.

Bulbine frutescens from Cape Province, South Africa, is a fibrous-rooted species with soft, rather fleshy leaves about 8 in. (20 cm) long in a very loose rosette. The raceme of many bright yellow flowers, or sometimes brownish orange or white, appears in late spring. It is of easy culture and offsets freely to form large clumps.

Bulbinopsis semibarbata comes from Australia. It has a fibrous rootstock and thin fleshy leaves in a lax rosette about 6 in. (15 cm) high. Several yellow flowers are held above the leaves in early spring.

Gasteria liliputana* from Cape Province, South Africa, has a spirally arranged rosette of dark green, glossy leaves with pointed tips, $2\frac{1}{2}$ in. (6 cm) long, which are banded with greenish white spots. The pinkish red flowers are on a long stalk in summer.

G. verrucosa* is a variable South African species. The tapering leaves up to 6 in. (15 cm) long are greyish green with numerous white tubercles, giving a roughened surface, and arranged in a semi-rosette. Reddish flowers are borne on a long arch-ing stem in early summer. Plants offset freely to form extensive mats (see p. 46).

Haworthia greenii comes from South Africa, the main habitat of the genus. It is a semi-prostrate plant which offsets from the base to make clumps. The small thick leaves are densely crowded on a stem some 6 in. (15 cm) long and covered in tubercles. The flowers are whitish, in summer.

H. reinwardtii,* with over 20 varieties, is similar to H. greenii. The greenish or brownish green leaves are densely arranged along the stem and mostly covered with many white protuberances.

H. retusa, another variable species, has a rosette made up of small, thick, fleshy leaves, triangular and slightly recurved, which are translucent with whitish green lines. It offsets freely from the base to form clumps.

Xanthorrhoea semiplana is a representative of a small Australian genus. It has a rosette of slender leaves well over $3\frac{1}{4}$ ft (1 m) long and a compact spike of white flowers on a stem which may be $6\frac{1}{2}$ ft (2 m) high. Plants can be grown from seed and, in cultivation, should remain "containable" for many years (see p. 13)!

44

Like most aloes, *A. distans* (left) is grown mainly for the handsome foliage; *Aloe variegata* (right) is unusual in having leaves arranged in ranks, not in a rosette

MESEMBRYANTHEMACEAE

This is a huge family containing over 100 genera and numerous species. Some are shrubby, others widespreading, and they include the so-called mimicry plants, such as *Lithops*, which model themselves on their surroundings. The majority are of fairly easy culture, but require care in judging when to water and when to allow them to dry out completely, since they differ in their needs. This aspect of growing "mesems" is critical: if water is given during the dormant season, plants tend to rot; equally, if they are left too dry during the growing and flowering seasons, they are liable to shrivel. (Individual requirements are indicated in the descriptions below.) Always give them the best possible light and grow in a very porous, but enriched compost with a minimum temperature of 50°F (10°C). The family is based in southern Africa, with a large number of species found in Cape Province. Propagation is easy from seeds or cuttings.

Aloinopsis schooneesii has a tuberous rootstock and small, thick, bluish green leaves grouped in a rough rosette. The flowers are bright yellow striped with red, in late summer and early autumn (see p. 46).
A. setifera forms a tiny rosette about 1¼ in. (3 cm) across. The leaves are triangular, short, thick and wide, the tips edged with minute teeth and tubercles. The flowers are bright yellow, sometimes pinkish. Both *Aloinopsis* species should be kept dry from November to late February.

Gasteria verrucosa (left) comes from South Africa, as do all members of the genus; *Aloinopsis schooneesii* (right) is dormant in winter, when no water should be given

*Carpobrotus acinaciformis** inhabits shady areas near Cape Town, South Africa. The stems are angled and branched with long, succulent, greyish green leaves. The flowers are about 4 in. (10 cm) across in rich carmine-purple, produced in late spring and early summer.

C. edulis is similar, but with longer stems and branches. The leaves are three-angled, up to 5½ in. (12 cm) long, fleshy and bright green. The flowers vary from pale yellow to reddish purple, in summer. Keep the plant fairly dry in winter and water when flower buds appear.

Cephalophyllum alstonii is a prostrate species with long greyish branches. The leaves, in tufts, are cylindrical with the upper surface flattened, greyish green and densely covered with minute, dark green, translucent dots. The flowers are a rich ruby red with distinctive violet stamens, in midsummer. Water from early March to October, but always in moderation.

Chasmatophyllum musculinum is a cushion-forming plant. The greyish or bluish green leaves are three-angled, the upper surface convex and the edges sometimes with minute teeth. The flowers are yellow, in late summer. Keep it dry from November to early March, then water carefully.

Cheiridopsis candidissima is a spreading plant, with leaves developing in pairs, greyish green, somewhat boat-shaped and generally covered with small, dark green dots. The flowers are yellow, in summer.

C. pillansii has small paired leaves, rounded on the outer surface, flat on the inner, which are silvery grey with minute dots of a deeper shade. Golden yellow flowers, about 2½ in. (6 cm) across, are borne on short fleshy stems in summer. Both species require watering from mid-February until November.

Conicosia capensis is a short-lived plant. The stems carry tufted heads of three-angled, green to bluish green leaves, 15 in. (40 cm) long. The flowers, about 2¾ in. (7 cm) across, are pale to canary-yellow.

C. pugioniformis is similar, having more erect stems and leaves greyish with reddish bases. The flowers, usually one to three together from the tops of the branches, are bright sulphur-yellow, in summer. Water these *Conicosia* species freely from April to late October.

Conophytum luisae has tiny heart-shaped bodies (consisting of two thick, united leaves), with short, rounded, greyish green lobes, edged with a darker shade, and the whole is covered with minute darker dots. The flowers are yellow.

C. pearsonii has cone-shaped bodies of glaucous green, with a central cleft which is almost closed and sometimes surrounded with dark dots. It is a beautiful plant, with deep lilac flowers produced in late summer. With all *Conophytum* species, a new body forms within the old body, gradually developing and being sustained by the old body, which eventually dries to leave only a skin. Watering should commence once the new body is apparent and cease by December; it should never be excessive.

Delosperma echinatum is a bushy, much branched plant, with thick, fleshy, bristly leaves. The flowers are white or creamy yellow and can appear at any time throughout the year, but mainly in summer. Water moderately from April to October.

Dorotheanthus bellidiformis* is the annual "mesembryanthemum", a very free-flowering plant often used for summer bedding in the garden. The alternate leaves are very fleshy and warty and the flowers appear in a variety of colours – white, pink, red, orange or multicoloured. Water regularly once growth is apparent. (It has now been reclassified in the genus *Cleretum*; see p. 48.)

Faucaria tuberculosa* is typical of many similar plants from Cape Province. The deep green leaves are very thick, about ¾ in. (2 cm) long and the same in width, roughly triangular and set with small teeth on the upper surface and margins. The flowers are pale yellow, about 1½ in. (4 cm) across, in late summer. Water with care from April to October.

Glottiphyllum linguiforme is a well-known species with thick, fleshy, bright green leaves and golden yellow flowers, about 2½ in. (6 cm) across, on short stalks.

G. oligocarpum has short stems bearing four leaves in two rows, thick, fleshy, greyish green and velvety. The flowers are yellow, in summer. Water both species carefully from late March to September.

Kensitia pillansii is one of the less common species from Cape Province. It is a many-branched shrub up to 2 ft (60 cm) tall, with reddish branches clad in three-angled, very succulent, slightly incurved leaves. The flowers are borne singly at the tips of the branches, about 2 in. (5 cm) across, with numerous widespreading petals of reddish purple and white. They appear in summer. It requires much the same treatment as *Lampranthus*.

Lampranthus albus is a semi-shrub about 8 in. (20 cm) high, with fleshy, bluish or bluish white leaves and pure white flowers.

L. aureus has longer, greenish grey leaves and brilliant orange flowers.

L. haworthii has long, fleshy, cylindrical leaves, which are densely grey-woolly. Lilac-purple flowers, up to 2½ in. (7 cm) across, are produced in profusion (see p. 48).

L. purpureus is a much-branched species with glaucous green leaves and purplish flowers (see p. 63).

L. roseus,* a popular species, has three-angled leaves covered with translucent dots and charming pale pink flowers about 1½ in. (4 cm) in diameter.

L. zeyheri has many curved slender branches with cylindrical leaves of bright green, which are enhanced by bright purple-violet flowers about 2½ in. (6 cm) across, borne singly at the tips of the branches. The *Lampranthus* species have some of the most colourful flowers in the family, produced in summer. All require a rest period from late October until March.

Lapidaria margaretae is less often encountered than other "mesems". The tiny leaves are united at the base, usually six to eight together on an extremely short, almost unnoticeable stem, and have a smooth whitish or pinkish surface with

Dorotheanthus bellidiformis (left) is a popular bedding plant, easily raised from seed sown in spring; *Lampranthus haworthii* (right) covers itself in flowers in summer

reddish margins. The flowers are bright golden yellow, about 2 in. (5 cm) across, in summer. It requires very careful watering and should be kept dry from late October till April.

Lithops julii has stone-like bodies of whitish grey, about ¾ in. (2 cm) across and gradually forming clumps. The top surface is grooved with brownish lines and dots and the flowers are pure white, about 1¼ in. (3 cm) wide. It belongs to one of the foremost genera in the family – commonly termed stone plants or living stones on account of their shape and normally having white or yellow flowers. The flowering period is from July to November and the flowers generally open in the afternoon. Give the plants good light and a porous compost and keep dry from December to late April.

L. karasmontana, another interesting and popular white-flowering species, has cone-shaped bodies which are very wrinkled on top.

*L. leslei** tends to become multi-headed quite quickly. The small bodies are brownish or reddish green, pitted with brownish and greenish markings and spots on the flat upper surface. The flowers are bright yellow.

*L. pseudotruncatella** and its varieties are very popular. They have conical, brownish grey bodies, covered with a network of marbling, veining and dots, which quickly form groups. The species has golden yellow flowers, while the variety *mundtii* has yellowish orange flowers about 1½ in. (4 cm) across, with red tips to the petals. In the variety *volkii* the bodies are usually arranged in groups of four, each about 1¼ in. (3 cm) wide, greyish blue with numerous dots of a deeper shade, and the flowers are yellow.

Nananthus aloides is a low-growing species with tapering, dark green leaves covered with numerous tubercles and having roughened edges, six to ten together in a basal tuft. The flowers are yellow, often with a deeper stripe on the petals, and about 1 in. (2.5 cm) across.

N. transvaalensis is similar, but with shorter leaves, and its dullish green background colour is emphasized by the prominent bumps along the margins. The

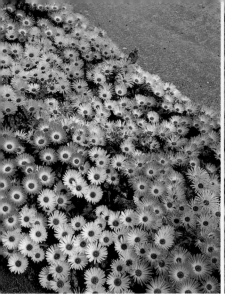

Lithops pseudotruncatella var. *volkii* (left), a widely grown stone or pebble plant; *Ophthalmophyllum latum* (right), a windowed plant which should be kept dry from December to late April

flowers are borne in summer and are bright yellow, each petal having a thin red line down the centre. Keep these two species completely dry from late October till April.

Ophthalmophyllum dinteri has cylindrical bodies up to 1½ in. (4 cm) high and about ¾ in. (2 cm) wide, with a deep cleft across the top, generally reddish green and the lobes having reddish transparent "windows". The flowers are reddish purple and about 1¼ in. (3 cm) wide.

O. latum is similar, the bodies being a pale yellowish green, with slightly warty lobes and deeper greenish dots around the area of the "windows". The flowers are pure white. These require the same attention as *Lithops*, to which they are closely related, and they flower in late summer and autumn.

Pleiospilos bolusii* has thick fleshy bodies consisting of one pair of leaves about 2¾ in. (7 cm) long, greyish green with numerous darker green dots covering the surface. The golden yellow flowers, 2½ in. (6 cm) or more across and often three or four together on short stems, are borne in late summer. Water freely when the plants are in full growth and then keep them dry.

Ruschia modesta grows about 18 in. (45 cm) tall, with long branches each bearing two boat-shaped leaves. The whole is finely covered with protuberances and the very small, deep purple flowers are borne on a short head in summer.

R. namaquana is some 6 in. (15 cm) high with several stiffish branches fairly densely covered with small, greenish, hairy, dotted leaves and many small white flowers.

R. utilis is one of the tallest members of this genus of shrubby plants, often attaining 6½ ft (2 m). It is bushy, with greyish stems and branches, which are densely leafy, and the flowerhead consists of numerous small white flowers. Keep it and its relatives dry from October to March.

Trichodiadema bulbosum has a pronounced tuberous rootstock which, if exposed, resembles the base of a bonsai tree. The stems reach about 8 in. (20 cm) high and the leaves are small, thick and fleshy, greyish green and minutely bristly. The deep crimson flowers are about ¾ in. (2 cm) across, in late autumn.

49

T. mirabile has stems covered with small bristle-like hairs and cylindrical leaves of bright green with small brownish bristles. The flowers are pure white. All species need only a short period of dormancy from late November to February and flower in late summer and early autumn.

MORACEAE

This interesting family, which includes the fig and mulberry, has just two truly succulent genera and these only in part. However, there are a few unusual succulent species, which are much in demand from connoisseurs. Plants require a rich porous compost, a minimum temperature of 59°F (15°C) and very careful watering, particularly for *Dorstenia*. The flowering time is summer. They can be grown quite successfully from seed or, in some instances, cuttings.

Dorstenia crispa from east Africa has fleshy, slightly swollen, semi-erect stems with a few short branches towards the tips. The leaves are hairy, narrowly tapering, with crisped edges, and some 2¾ in. (7 cm) long. The petalless flower is set on a star-shaped base about ¾ in. (2 cm) across with thickened edges and longer bracts.
D. hildebrandtii develops a small caudex with thickish stems and branches and broadly spear-shaped leaves. The flowers appear from the leaf axils and have a purplish base with deeper purple bracts.
Ficus decaisnei from the Philippines is one of several Far Eastern epiphytic species which can be considered succulent (although the genus is better known for the fig, *F. carica*, and rubber plant, *F. elastica*). It has elliptical fleshy leaves and elongated aerial roots which eventually reach ground level to form bush-like plants.
F. palmeri from Mexico is a tree-like species, although seldom exceeding 3¼ ft (1 m) in cultivation, with a thick caudex-type base and oval downy leaves about 2¾ in. (7 cm) long and 2 in. (5 cm) across. Insignificant whitish flowers are followed by fig-like fruits. When young, it makes an excellent houseplant.

PASSIFLORACEAE

Only one genus in this family, which includes the popular passion flower, contains known succulents. They differ from other members of the family in having a caudex-like base, resembling that of a bonsai tree. A fairly rich, porous compost is advised and water can be applied freely while plants are in growth, but must be withheld during the dormant season. They flower in summer. Give good light and an airy position with a minimum temperature of 50°F (10°C). They are easily grown from seed or cuttings.

Adenia globosa from Kenya has a large stone-like caudex developing several thick erect branches, which are greyish green and spiny. Leaves appear infrequently and, when they do, soon fall. The scented flowers are star-like and bright red.
A. pechuelii from Namibia has a large, fleshy, greenish grey caudex, somewhat bottle-shaped, and many branches with spines. The pale pink flowers are produced in clusters of three at the top.

PEDALIACEAE

A number of genera in this family include succulent species, but only the southern African *Pterodiscus* has achieved any degree of popularity. They are mainly low-growing and given careful attention, can become very interesting, attractive, flowering plants. A temperature of 55°F (13°C) is advisable, a bright location and careful watering, keeping them completely dry during dormancy. They flower in summer. A rich porous compost, totally lime-free, is necessary. They are easily grown from seed.

Pterodiscus luridus has a rounded caudex, 2 in. (5 cm) or more thick, very fleshy and tapering to a branched point. The plant rarely exceeds 18 in. (45 cm). The numerous leaves along the branches are dark green above, bluish white and woolly below. The flowers are yellow dotted with red.

P. speciosus is seldom more than 6 in. (15 cm) tall. The narrow leaves have toothed edges and the slender funnel-shaped flowers are pale purplish red (see p. 52).

PORTULACACEAE

This is a family of beautiful colourful plants, many of them popular in the garden and others used for greenhouse and home decoration. They include annuals and perennials and the majority can be easily increased from seeds or cuttings. A sunny position is essential for best results and the compost or soil should be rich, open and free from lime. The perennial species require a fairly dry dormant period, but a little water can be given occasionally if the temperature is maintained above 55°F (13°C). They flower in summer.

Anacampseros alstonii is one of the most fascinating species. The base is a flat thick caudex 2½ in. (6 cm) or so in diameter, from the top of which numerous short fleshy stems emerge, bearing rows of small leaves almost totally concealed in a sheath of silvery white. The flowers protrude well beyond the stems and are pure white. It is an exceedingly choice miniature.

A. australiana from Australia is one of the very few species found outside the African continent. It has a long, thick, tuberous rootstock, with much of the stem underground. The small lance-shaped leaves in a basal rosette are hairy, whitish and very succulent and the flowers are bright pink.

A. rufescens* from the Karroo, South Africa, has a thick, tuberous, caudex-like rootstock with many erect and spreading stems and branches about 2½ in. (6 cm) long. The thick, spirally arranged leaves are green on the upper surface, reddish below, with yellowish white, bristly hairs almost as long as the leaves. The flowers are deep pink.

Calandrinia grandiflora from Chile grows nearly 3¼ ft (1 m) tall when in full bloom. The oval leaves with pointed tips are green and fleshy, up to 6 in. (15 cm) long and mostly at the base of the plant. The small flowers are bright pale purple, borne in terminal clusters.

The dwarf *Pterodiscus speciosus* (left) requires full exposure to sun;
the popular *Lewisia cotyledon* hybrids (right) are available in a wide
range of colours

C. polyandra occurs in many parts of Australia. Up to 20 in. (50 cm) tall, it has
several erect stems with succulent, greyish green leaves and racemes of deep pink
flowers.

Lewisia cotyledon is from northern California. The species and its many hybrids
are well known in cultivation, usually being treated as alpines. The leaves are
arranged in a basal rosette about 4½ in. (12 cm) in diameter and may be quite fleshy
or softer, with or without toothed margins. The flowers in panicles on stems 4 in.
(10 cm) long are white or pink and veined in shades of red. The Sunset strain is one
of the best. Lewisias do well if planted on their sides in a wall and are easily propagated from the plentiful seed.

L. rediviva is similar, with a long, tapering, fleshy rootstock which is said to be
edible, narrow fleshy leaves and large white flowers.

*Portulaca grandiflora** – or, rather, its hybrids – is commonly grown in gardens as a
half-hardy annual and is available in a vast array of colours with both single and
double flowers. The true species is found in the Windward Islands of the
Caribbean; it is widespreading with slender leaves and has red single or double
flowers on 6 in. (15 cm) stems. The sun plants, as they are sometimes called, thrive
in rather poor, dry soil (see also p. 2).

*Portulacaria afra** from South Africa is a shrubby plant with many branches. The
leaves are small, glossy green and almost circular and, like the stems and branches,
are obviously succulent. The very small, inconspicuous flowers are pinkish. There
is also an attractive variegated form.

VITACEAE

The succulent species of this family originate mainly from Africa,
including Madagascar, and many have a caudiciform base, which
has helped to account for their popularity. The flowers, borne in
summer, are less interesting than the fruits. These resemble
grapes (grapevine is a member of the family), but are usually

The annual *Portulaca grandiflora* (left) opens its flowers only in a sunny position; the variegated form of *Portulacaria afra* (right) makes an attractive foliage houseplant

smaller in size and in the number of fruits to a cluster. A really porous compost is essential and preferably one rich in humus. Plants need a bright, not necessarily sunny position and should be freely watered during the growing season, but kept completely dry during dormancy. A minimum temperature of 50°F (10°C) is required.

*Cissus quadrangularis** from east Africa is well known and has climbing four-angled stems with wing-like edges. The stems are divided into segments and the leaves appear at the nodes, being thick, three-lobed and with toothed margins. The fruits are black.

Cyphostemma seitziana has grape-like fruits

C. rotundifolia is from the Transvaal and also known in Saudi Arabia. It has more rounded leaves with smooth edges and the fruits are green, becoming red.

Cyphostemma bainesii from Namibia has a bottle-shaped caudex about 10 in. (25 cm) thick and 2 ft (60 cm) tall and a few stout branches towards the top, the whole enveloped in a greenish skin. The leaves are about 4½ in. (12 cm) long and covered with minute hairs.

C. seitziana is a taller species and has long, oval, fleshy, greyish green leaves with serrated margins. The fruits are yellowish becoming reddish (see p. 53).

Mother-in-law's tongue, *Sansevieria trifasciata* var. *laurentii*, has long been grown as a houseplant

Pests and diseases

Most pests and diseases can be conveniently dealt with by applying suitable pesticides and fungicides, which are available under various trade names.

PESTS

As a preventive measure, treat plants with insecticide two or three times a year during the growing season, always ensuring the soil gets a thorough soaking. If, however, they are already infested, an aerosol spray can be very effective; the treatment should be repeated at intervals of five to seven days until all signs of the pests are gone, followed by a thorough overhead spray with slightly tepid water, to wash away dead insects which might still remain on stems or leaves.

The pests most likely to be encountered are comparatively few, but all can prove a danger unless destroyed.

Mealybug

These small insects are covered with a whitish waxy substance. They lay their eggs in rather concealed places, always in clusters, and these too have a white waxy-woolly coating. One method of dealing speedily with them is to take a stiff paint brush, dip it in methylated spirits and remove the waxy coating on the insects and eggs, without which they will not survive. Then, after a thorough cleansing with tepid water sprayed overhead, treat with malathion to help avoid further infestations.

Root mealybug

This pest is less easy to detect and the tendency is for plants to be attacked during the dormant season. If they suggest poor growth or become weary-looking or fail to flower, there is every reason to suspect something is wrong at the roots. Carefully remove the plant from its pot and you may discern a lot of whitish "mould" adhering to both the soil and the inner surface of the pot. This is wax secreted by root mealybug. The whole lot can be washed away with tepid water containing malathion and the plant should be repotted in fresh compost. Towards the end of the growing season, give a good application of malathion, standing the pot in the solution until the compost is really saturated, and then allow the soil to dry out for the period of dormancy.

Scale insects

These tiny sap-feeding pests have a limpet-like shell covering of brownish or greyish brown. When they reach adult stage, they cease to move. Eggs are laid and hatched under the shell or scale and the resulting larvae seek a suitable feeding area and themselves become immobile. They can be carefully scraped away or, when the scales are newly hatched, may be removed with a soft cloth dipped in methylated spirits. Alternatively, the use of a spray containing malathion will be very satisfactory.

Whitefly and aphids

These are persistent and dangerous pests with certain succulents. Several commercially produced sprays are available and can be used for indoor plants, while in the greenhouse gamma-HCH smokes are always effective. Some modern sprays and smokes contain permethrin, which can be recommended to repel attacks of whitefly and pernicious aphids such as greenfly. Whitefly can also be controlled by introducing the parasitic chalcid wasp, *Encarsia formosa*.

Red spider mite

These minute reddish pests colonize and surround themselves with very fine webs. They feed from the stems and leaves by piercing the skin and sucking the sap, frequently causing discolouration of the plant generally. Since they appear to flourish in a dry atmosphere, reasonable humidity plus good ventilation should afford protection and discourage the pests. Sprays containing malathion or pirimiphos-methyl can be used to deal with attacks. Biological control with the predatory mite, *Phytoseiulus persimilis*, is an effective alternative (Addresses of suppliers of biological controls are available from the entomologist at the RHS Garden, Wisley).

Sciarid fly

Also known as mushroom fly, these pests have become more prevalent with the popularity of peat-based composts. The minute greyish white flies lay their eggs in the compost, which hatch out into thin whitish grubs and feed on the roots of seedlings and mature plants alike. Insecticides containing malathion or per-methrin are recommended as sprays, while diazinon granules can be mixed with the compost.

Vine weevil

These grubs are plump white maggots with light brown heads, up to ½ in. (1 cm) long. They live in the soil, where they destroy roots and bore into the base of succulents, especially in the autumn to spring period. The adults are slow-moving dull black beetles, which are active at night during the spring and summer. The older grubs are difficult to control as they are tolerant of most pesticides. Plants can be given protection by drenching the compost with gamma-HCH or permethrin in early July and early August. Look for and destroy adult weevils hiding under pots, leaves and greenhouse staging, particularly during the spring and early summer. Infested plants should be repotted in fresh compost, although the root damage may be so severe that it is better to propagate new plants from cuttings. Fortunately, this destructive pest very rarely attacks succulents.

DISEASES

Diseases with succulents are mainly confined to black rot and damping off, the latter being largely a problem with seedlings.

Black rot

This is likely to be in evidence with many of the Asclepiadaceae, such as *Stapelia* and kindred genera. A blackening of the stem becomes apparent at more or less soil level, which is caused by bacteria penetrating the stems and turning the tissues black and soft. If noted at an early stage, the affected parts can be cut away with a sharp knife and the cut area dusted with flowers of sulphur or dry bordeaux powder. Any good copper-based fungicide used as a spray will help to control and possibly prevent the problem occurring.

Damping off

This can be prevented by the use of a good fungicide, cheshunt compound being a well-proven antidote. Mix it with water and lightly spray seedlings at the first watering following germination.

Orbea (Stapelia) variegata is one of the commonest members of the Asclepiadaceae

The fact must never be overlooked that pesticides and fungicides are poisonous. Always handle them with extreme care, use only as instructed on the container and, above all, keep them out of reach of children and pets. Some succulents may be damaged by pesticides. Avoid treating plants while they are exposed to bright sunlight or high temperatures or are very dry at the roots.

Further information

SUPPLIERS

Chiltern Seeds, Bortree Stile, Ulverston, Cumbria LA12 7PB (seeds only)
Holly Gate Nurseries, Ashington, West Sussex RH20 3BA
Mesa Garden, D. Rushforth, 32 Trafalgar Rd, Birkdale, Southport PR8 2EX (seeds only)
Oak Dene Nurseries, 10 Back Lane West, Royston, Barnsley, Yorks S71 4SB
Southfield Nurseries, Louth Rd, Holton-le-Clay, Grimsby DN36 5HL
Southwest Seeds, 200 Spring Rd, Kempston, Bedford MK42 8ND (seeds only)
Westfield Cactus, Kennford, Exeter EX6 7XD
Whitestone Gardens Ltd, Sutton-under-Whitestonecliffe, Thirsk, Yorks YO7 2PZ
Windyridge Nursery, Burford Garden Centre, Shilton Rd, Burford, Oxon OZ8 4NZ

RECOMMENDED READING

Aloes of South Africa, G.W. Reynolds. Balkema, Cape Town, 1969.
Aloes of Tropical Africa and Madagascar, G.W. Reynolds. The Trustees, The Aloes Book Fund, Swaziland, 1969.
Aloes, Barbara Jeppe. Purnell, Cape Town, 1974.
Echeveria, Eric Walther. California Academy of Sciences, San Francisco, 1972.
The New Haworthia Handbook, Bruce Bayer. National Botanic Gardens of SA, Cape Town, 1982.
Haworthia and Astroloba, John Pilbeam. Batsford, London, 1983.
Handbook of Cultivated Sedums, Ronald Evans. Science Reviews Ltd, Northwood, Middlesex, 1983.
Lexicon of Succulent Plants, Hermann Jacobsen. Blandford Press, Poole, Dorset, 1977.
Ashingtonia, Vol. 1/2. Holly Gate International Ltd, Sussex.
Succulent Flora of Southern Africa, Doreen Court. Balkema, Rotterdam, 1981.
Illustrated Encyclopedia of Succulents, Gordon Rowley. Salamander, London, 1978.
Handbook of Succulent Plants, 3 vols, Hermann Jacobsen. Blandford Press, London, 1960.

SOCIETIES

British Cactus and Succulent Society, Membership Secretary, 23 Linden Leas, West Wickham, Kent BR4 0SE.

The Madagascan palm, *Pachypodium lamerei*, is a striking plant but not difficult to grow

Hoya carnosa 'Tricolor' (above) and *Hoya purpurea-fusca* (below) both need a semi-shaded position

Index of genera

Adenia 50
Adenium 28
Adromischus 35
Aeonium 35–6
Agave 25–6
Aloe 43–4
Aloinopsis 45
Anacampseros 51

Bulbine 44
Bulbinopsis 44

Calandrinia 51–2
Calibanus 26
Caralluma 28–9
Carpobrotus 46
Cephalophyllum 46
Ceropegia 29
Chasmatophyllum 46
Cheiridopsis 46
Cissus 53–4
Cleretum 47
Conicosia 46–7
Conophytum 47
Coreopsis 33
Cotyledon 36
Crassula 36–7
Cyanotis 33
Cyphostemma 54

Delosperma 47
Dorotheanthus 47
Dorstenia 50
Dracaena 26
Dudleya 37
Duvalia 29–30

Echeveria 37
Euphorbia 41

Faucaria 47
Ficus 50

Gasteria 44
Gerrardanthus 40
Glottiphyllum 47
Graptopetalum 37

Haworthia 44
Hoodia 30
Hoya 30
Huernia 31

Ipomoea 34

Jatropha 41

Kalanchoe 37–8
Kedrostis 40
Kensitia 47
Kleinia 33

Lampranthus 47
Lapidaria 47–8
Lewisia 52
Lithops 48
Luckhoffia 31

Nananthus 48–9

Ophthalmophyllum 49
Orbea 31
Othonna 33

Pachyphytum 38–9
Pachypodium 28
Pedilanthus 41
Pelargonium 43
Pleiospilos 49

Plumiera 28
Portulaca 52
Portulacaria 52
Pterodiscus 51

Ruschia 49

Sansevieria 26–7
Sarcocaulon 43
Sedum 39–40
Sempervivum 40

Senecio 33–4
Stapelia 31–2

Trichocaulon 32
Tradescantia 33
Trichodiadema 49–50
Tridentea 32
Tripogandra 33
Turbina 34

Xanthorrhoea 44

Yucca 27

The vivid purple flowers of *Lampranthus purpureus* appear in summer